Red Pandas

Julie Murray

Abdo Kids Junior
is an Imprint of Abdo Kids
abdobooks.com

Abdo
Kids

INTERESTING ANIMALS

abdobooks.com

Published by Abdo Kids, a division of ABDO, P.O. Box 398166, Minneapolis, Minnesota 55439.
Copyright © 2023 by Abdo Consulting Group, Inc. International copyrights reserved in all countries.
No part of this book may be reproduced in any form without written permission from the publisher.
Abdo Kids Junior™ is a trademark and logo of Abdo Kids.

Printed in the United States of America, North Mankato, Minnesota.

102022

012023

 THIS BOOK CONTAINS RECYCLED MATERIALS

Photo Credits: Alamy, Getty Images, Minden Pictures, Shutterstock

Production Contributors: Teddy Borth, Jennie Forsberg, Grace Hansen

Design Contributors: Candice Keimig, Pakou Moua

Library of Congress Control Number: 2022937166

Publisher's Cataloging-in-Publication Data

Names: Murray, Julie, author.

Title: Red pandas / by Julie Murray

Description: Minneapolis, Minnesota : Abdo Kids, 2023 | Series: Interesting animals | Includes online
    resources and index.

Identifiers: ISBN 9781098264161 (lib. bdg.) | ISBN 9781098264727 (ebook) | ISBN 9781098265007
    (Read-to-Me ebook)

Subjects: LCSH: Red panda--Juvenile literature. | Lesser panda--Juvenile literature. | Animals--Juvenile
    literature. | Zoology--Juvenile literature.

Classification: DDC 599.763--dc23

Table of Contents

Red Pandas

Red pandas live in Asia. They are mainly found in the mountains.

North America
Europe
Asia
Africa
South America
Australia
N
E
W
S

5

Red pandas can grow up to 2 feet (61 cm) long. They weigh up to 17 pounds (7.7 kg).

They have reddish fur. Their

legs and belly are black.

Their head is round. Their face and ears have white fur.

They have a long tail.

The tail has stripes.

Red pandas can stand on their hind legs. They do this when they feel scared.

15

They have **padded** feet.

Their claws are sharp!

They are good climbers.
They spend most of their
time in trees.

They eat **bamboo**.

They also eat berries
and eggs.

Red Panda Features

long tail

red and black body fur

sharp claws

white markings on
face and ears

Glossary

bamboo

a tropical grass plant that has hard, woody, hollow stems.

padded

covered in a soft material for protection. A red panda's paws are covered in hair.

Index

Abdo Kids
ONLINE
FREE! ONLINE MULTIMEDIA RESOURCES

Visit **abdokids.com** to access crafts, games, videos, and more!

Use Abdo Kids code

IRK4161

or scan this QR code!